I0414253

AMERICAN

FASCISM

HOW TO VOTE AGAINST THE

CORPORATE OLIGARCHY

Illustration by RJ Matson

<u>Contents</u>

Re-Educating America

The information provided in this handbook should act as a guide to who controls the United States Government, while providing a brief explanation of their motives. The opinions presented are not meant to serve as biased propaganda and are aimed specifically at promoting an agenda of truth. For many years the American media and politicians from both liberal and conservative sides have fostered a false narrative that capitalism is synonymous with "Free Market". We are taught that capitalism is the central vehicle of democracy and the sole catalyst of innovation, job creation, wealth production, and the protector of personal liberty. However, this blatant coloring of political ideology is a direct threat to American values. In an attempt to reverse this intentional misinformation we will evaluate the ideology of governments throughout history and their underlying motives in order to map out their fundamental differences so that as a society we can be better prepared to vote against any oppressive administration. If you come across any words you do not understand, reference the glossary at the end of the book. All data and research has been compiled and cross-referenced from various reputable resources, yet, no citations are provided with the intent that you research, discover, refute, or validate this commentary yourself.

The most important democratic strategy above all is the encouragement of civil discussion, followed by the pursuit of human progress...

The Worship of Capitalism: How is America Fascist Oligarchy?

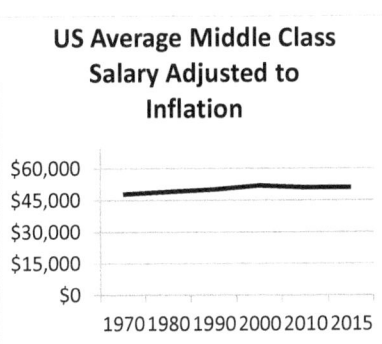

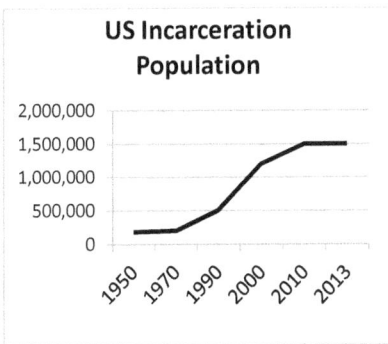

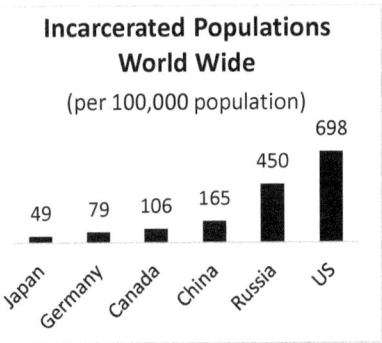

Oligarchy: a small group that exercises control especially for corrupt and selfish purposes in any type of government.

Government is a system by which a state or society is controlled that attempts to address the needs, protection and general management of that community. To understand how America became an Oligarchy, even though we have a democratic system, we have to understand the characteristics that separate democratic and authoritarian societies. Democracies attempt to meet the needs of the community while protecting personal liberty as much as possible, whereas authoritarian societies disregard personal liberty for the betterment of the community as a whole. America has two major political parties: democratic (liberal, socialistic) and republican (conservative, capitalistic). Many people agree that the principle objective of government should be to uphold liberty. This core philosophy is commonly associated with Libertarianism. What has been lost is that while the same person can identify as conservative or liberal on different topics, our two party system and the corporate media has forced us to choose sides .This division has eliminated the power of the people to come to an effective compromise; a phenomenon sometimes referred to as "Polarized Pluralism". While millions of Americans believe the "American Dream" is dying and that economically, morally, and culturally, we are losing site of the principles that once embodied the American spirit, a political conversation often ends with friends, family and otherwise harmless acquaintances hating each other which ultimately diminishes the power of the voter base and allows authoritarians to be elected.

> *"However, political parties may now and then answer popular ends, they are likely in the course of time and things, to become potent engines, by which cunning, ambitious, and unprincipled men will be enabled to subvert the power of the people and to usurp for themselves the reins of government, destroying afterwards the very engines which have lifted them to unjust dominion." – George Washington,*
> *Independent Revolutionary and 1st President of United States*

<u>Setting the Record Straight</u>

To further understand how a society slides into a public or private authoritarianism, we must consider the methods that drive the policies of opposing ideologies and how they exploit the populations that identify within them.

The history of political ideologies and how they relate to a governments control structure gives us insight to the viability of those options, and their effects on personal liberty. Over time two basic ideological oppositions formed: liberal and conservative. The parallels between these two major ideologies stem throughout every political situation in the history of the world. Fascist leaders like Mussolini and Adolf Hitler, Communist dictators like Mao Zedong and Fidel Castro, American presidents and social leaders all fall somewhere between these two basic philosophies. This is called the Political Spectrum. There are many complexities and nuances between similar distinctions; however, for the purpose of this guide I have simplified it to make it easier to understand the big picture. If you look at the illustration below, liberal and conservative ideologies are on opposite sides of the spectrum and as you move further towards the outside the control structure becomes progressively more authoritarian, while the more moderate, democratic methods are closer to the center. The anti-authoritarian, utopian ideologies have been included at the bottom as well, which we will expose later.

The Political Spectrum

Liberal (Left Wing)			Conservative (Right Wing)		
Socialistic			Capitalistic		
Authoritarian Communism	Democratic Socialism	Libertarian Socialism	Libertarian Conservatism	Democratic Capitalism	Authoritarian Fascism
Authoritarian		Democratic			Authoritarian
Anarcho-Communism (Utopian)			Anarcho-Capitalism (Utopian)		

Often confused, communism is the inverse opposite of fascism. Communism is a liberal ideology with a socialistic method, whereas fascism is conservative and capitalistic. Mussolini, who is known as the "Father of modern Fascism", confirms this in his 1931 essay entitled *The Doctrine of Fascism* when he writes "*Fascism is definitely and absolutely opposed to the doctrines of liberalism, both in the political and economic sphere*". He goes on to say "*Fascism is therefore opposed to socialism to which unity within the state is unknown, and which sees in history nothing but the class struggle*". In fascism, the class struggle is ignored in favor of social Darwinism and the elite are idolized and empowered. While fascism is an exclusionary private tyranny, communism is an all encompassing welfare state. Socialism and capitalism are the driving methodologies in either of these forms of government, and the overuse of either, fueled by the division of the population between them, will always result in the rise of a more authoritarian style of government.

In the graphs at the beginning of the chapter I've shown you how the incarcerated population has nearly tripled in 30 years, and how in that same time, employee wages have stagnated as CEO salaries have exploded, and while productivity has increased, the wealth of the middle class has been redistributed to the top of our economic food chain. All of these things should signal as red flags to the destruction of liberty, but through propaganda, many have been blinded.

There is one concept that every person, regardless of their political affiliation or philosophies, has not discovered as the key to the conundrum of political warfare…

Balance…

The democratic balance between capitalistic industries and effective socioeconomic policy (socialism) is what creates a free market for people of all classes…

Utopias Do Not Exist

At this point one usually runs into the anarchist argument. The typical capitalism-loving American, usually a conservative libertarian, says "taxation is theft" or "without a state, private companies couldn't control the government". This brings us to the concept of Anarcho-Capitalism and inversely Anarcho-Communism. Like their authoritarian cousins, fascism and communism, one favors private ownership while the other calls for public ownership, both however, with the absence of the state. Neither of these systems are realistic because of the differences in what people are able, willing, or required to do in order to make a society work. Without central planning, industry cannot be effectively regulated and collective infrastructure, justice, health, and education systems cannot be adequately established. Stateless societies have never existed for a significant amount of time because they are overtaken by another organized state. It is vital to realize that democracy is threatened when a state is demonized rather than scrutinized as voters become disenfranchised and corporate leaders are easily elected.

Socialism Demonized

Socialism: a political and economic theory of social organization that advocates that the means of production, distribution, and exchange should be owned or regulated by the community as a whole.

Even though socialism is a neutral word that fundamentally aligns itself with Democracy, the American media machine has rendered a negative association with the term. Certain periods in history known as "red scares" came out of fear that a communist revolution would spread to America after the Russian Revolution in 1917, when the working class rose to defeat Emperor Nicholas II. The Second Red Scare came in reaction to World War II when the notorious Adolf Hitler and his "National Socialist German Workers Party" (Nazis) took power. Contrary to popular belief, Nazism is a right wing ideology and they actually executed anyone from socialist, communist and otherwise liberal factions. National socialists weren't all calling themselves fascists yet because the fascist movement had just begun. This simple misunderstanding is still heavily disputed everyday in America. Franklin Delano Roosevelt, a self-proclaimed Democratic Socialist and the 32nd American President, restored the promise of the American Dream after the Great Depression with socialist legislation known as the New Deal. After the stock market crash of 1929 Roosevelt established workers rights and infrastructure initiatives as well as other economic and social reforms that built up the middle class and eventually turned the economy around. Conservative critics of the New Deal claim that Roosevelt's plan prolonged the recession ignoring how his contribution to workers rights regulations and infrastructure built a strong middle class that would establish modern American consumerism. He also received criticism from the left as being too corporatist, which really underscores the struggle for compromise that exists within the political spectrum. Regardless, the New Deal was eventually successful illustrating a common theme throughout history where deregulation, cronyism and reckless profiteering in the name of capitalism eventually causes an economy to crash and socialistic policy is used to restore the market and balance corruption without the need for a violent workers revolution as famously described by Karl Marx.

"Private capital tends to become concentrated in a few hands, partly because of competition among the capitalists, and partly because of technological development and the increasing division of labor encourage the formation of larger units of production at the expense of the smaller ones. The result of these developments is an oligarchy of private capital, the enormous power of which cannot be effectively checked even by a democratically organized political society This is true since the members of legislative bodies are selected by political parties, largely financed or otherwise influenced by private capitalists who, for all practical purposes, separate the electorate from the legislature. The consequence is that the representatives of the people do not in fact sufficiently protect the interests of the underprivileged sections of the population. Moreover, under existing conditions, private capitalists inevitably control, directly or indirectly, the main sources of information (press, radio, education). It is thus extremely difficult, and indeed in most cases quite impossible, for the individual citizen to come to objective conclusions and to make intelligent use of his political rights." – Albert Einstein, Philosopher and Theoretical Physicist

Now that we have touched on the fundamental differences between capitalism and socialism, fascism and communism, and even utopian fantasies from both sides of the political spectrum, you should understand liberty cannot be protected without effective democratic implementation of both socialism and capitalism. The only viable system of government that does not forfeit personal liberty for the betterment of the population, and does not forfeit industry at the expense of economic equality is a mixture economy.

Let's dive a little deeper into how America became what it is today...

7

Economics: The Relationship between Industry and Community

US Minimum Wage Adjusted to Inflation

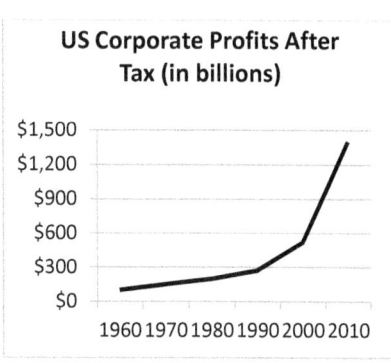

US Corporate Profits After Tax (in billions)

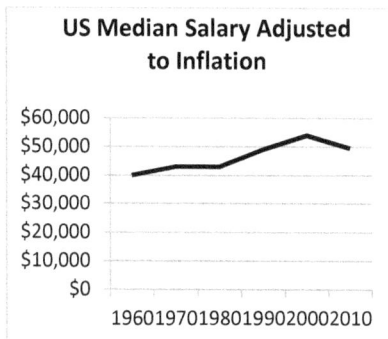

US Median Salary Adjusted to Inflation

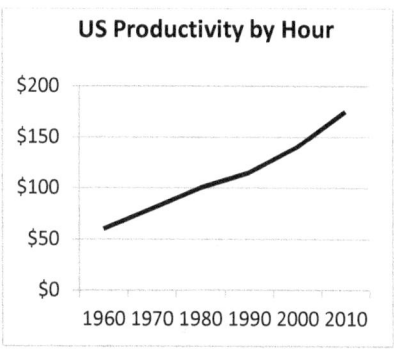

US Productivity by Hour

Fascism: the indirect control of a community by an elite group through private ownership of the means to production and exclusive social policy.

While the working class and many business owners identify our market as "Freer" under private control of industry, in many ways this belief has lead to a system controlled by an elite group of unelected plutocrats. Economists the world over study the effects of policy on industry hoping to unlock the secret to what makes an economy successful and sustainable. Supply and demand, opportunity cost, scarcity, etc are great theories to use when figuring out the decisions of individuals or companies within an economic construct, but what's often forgotten is that any structure is only as strong as its weakest link. The working class makes up the consumer base by creating demand and operating the means through which that demand is met.

The Federal Reserve: Infinite Debt Machine

The Federal Reserve is a system of 12 private banks that control the monetary policy in America. This exclusive network prints money and loans it to all the smaller banks at an interest rate with absolutely no physical commodity as a counterweight and virtually no public transparency. You see, debt is created at the very top of the financial pyramid. This is an infinite debt machine that promotes inflation. Inflation dictates how much purchasing power our currency has, which is why the minimum wage must be automatically raised and tied to inflation to offset currency devaluation, otherwise, the buying power is stripped from the working consumer as prices go up and wages do not. In turn, less capital is cycled through the economy.

"If the American people ever allow private banks to control the issue of their currency, first by inflation, then by deflation, the banks and corporations that will grow up around them will deprive the people of all property until their children wake up homeless on the continent their Fathers conquered." – Thomas Jefferson, United States President and Principal Author of the Declaration of Independence

An Inflated Sense of Wealth

Inflation: a general increase in prices and fall in the purchasing value of money.

In America there is an unrealistic measure of wealth. Someone who has a car and a house is viewed as acceptably successful, when they may have copious amounts of student debt, a loan for their car, an upside down mortgage, or any combination of economic burdens that don't translate to any tangible accumulation

9

of wealth. In a recent pew survey 80% of Americans admitted they are burdened by debt, and 70% of those same people said they could not afford their lifestyle without the active use of debt. This is really the norm, and our worship of wealth within our culture really points to our deep seeded longing for economic relief, stability, and through that, social acceptance. Meanwhile, our currency is not backed by any real asset or tied to any market variable, which is the reason the value of the dollar continues to shrink, and why inflation is continually created by the Federal Reserve. Worse still, in America only 7.4% of all money exists in physical form.

The Private Domination of Industry

Arguably the one of the biggest contributors to our rampant under-employment is Conglomeration. Conglomerates are giant companies that purchase or invest in many smaller companies with little or no vested interest in their product or service. They condense the workforce and undercut smaller competition resulting in market domination. "Free Trade" agreements have allowed many of these companies to move their operations out of the country to take advantage of populations with less workers rights and to avoid taxes. A popular example is the multinational corporation Berkshire Hathaway who owns or has holdings in Geico, BNSF Railway, Fruit of the Loom, Helzberg Diamonds, Net Jets, American Express, Coca-Cola, Wells Fargo, IBM, Mars INC... the list goes on. Every industry in America is under threat of market conglomeration which reduces the workforce and degrades the quality of American products and services.

Complication of Tax Codes

The subject of business regulation confuses many well meaning small business advocates due to the exploitation of tax loopholes by corporations and their manipulation of tax codes against small businesses through lobbying and cronyism. This leads many to believe that government kills small business through regulation and has been commonly referred to as "Crony-capitalism" and is even confused with socialism when it is really National Socialism, corporatism. A fascist, indirectly controlled government, lobbied by big business will not write regulations favoring small businesses. This causes a misguided distrust of government all together, which in turn, also aides the private oligarchy in becoming more powerful.

10

Trickledown Economics

Trickledown economics or "Reaganomics" is a group of conservative ideas that says the controllers of industry create demand, and subsequently, regulate workforce participation by creating jobs; tax cuts and protections from other policies benefiting the wealthy "trickle down" in the form of raises or employment opportunities and profits are shared with employees based on merit without any interference from government. This is a complete sham. When profits accumulate at the top of the economic food chain, they are reinvested in the company, saved, reported as gains to stock holders and otherwise excluded from re-entering the economy to be exchanged in local businesses, thereby re-distributing wealth away from the working consumer class and the small business market. Capitalism requires capital to exchange hands through individuals and businesses to work.

"Once you realize that trickle-down economics does not work, you will see the excessive tax cuts for the rich as what they are -- a simple upward redistribution of income, rather than a way to make all of us richer, as we were told." – Ha-joon Chang, Economist, Cambridge University

How Collective Bargaining Combats Government Wage Manipulation

Collective Bargaining is when workers from each respective industry together negotiate the terms and conditions of their employment; typically facilitated by a union. With the implementation of "Right to Work" and other anti-union legislation, union efforts have been limited and even eliminated in some states. We have devalued the American worker now that the employee is expendable in the unprincipled pursuit of profit and, as a result, devalued the quality of our products and services as well. The corporate establishment has the population convinced that higher wages hurt small business when in fact, large corporations need cheap labor to survive and are able to dominate a market weakened by a struggling consumer population. The only way to reverse the effects of this redistribution of wealth away from the working consumer class is to raise the minimum wage for all workers across all industries.

<u>The Minimum Wage Myth</u>

In order to combat inflation and lost purchasing power, minimum wage must be increased to protect an economy's sustainability. While the idea of a 15$ minimum wage by 2020 scares even moderate liberals it is nothing to fear. Here's some simple math for a small business with 5 full-time employees with an immediate 10$ wage increase: Let's say the boss makes 35$ per hour and employees make 8$. With no extra profit the business needs $3000 per week to cover payroll. Each employee's wages increase by 80$ per week under the new minimum wage. That's an extra $400 a week needed to pay the 5 employees. Most studies and examples of other countries with higher average minimum wages indicate the costs of goods and services will rise by 5-15%. If prices are raised by 10% at our fictional company that means a 50$ product is now 55$ which will raise our $3000 payroll allocation by an extra 300$ a week naturally, resulting in a very small change (less than 4%) in payroll costs. This small increase can be easily offset with increases in productivity, proper training/hiring/firing, a 2 hour reduction per employee (they still make an extra 60$ per week) or even a temporary decrease in administrative salaries (remember the CEO to Employee pay graph on page 2?) An estimated 15 million American workers make under 10$ per hour. As more consumers make more money all workers see increased wages with the influx of capital in the system. Large corporations currently controlling the market that survive off mass underemployment will scale down creating more quality jobs in the small business sector. Low wage workers have to make enough to contribute to the economy and stay off government assistance. Wal-mart workers alone receive over 6 billion dollars a year (almost a million per store) in government assistance.

I do not regard Socialism as a gospel of proletarian revenge, nor even, primarily, as a means of securing economic justice. I regard it primarily as an adjustment to machine production demanded by considerations of common sense"- **Bertrand Russell**, *Philosopher and Mathematician*

Health Care: Economic Liability? or Intangible Commodity?

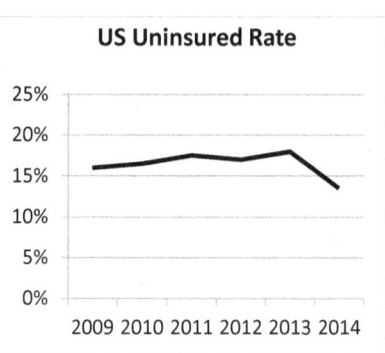

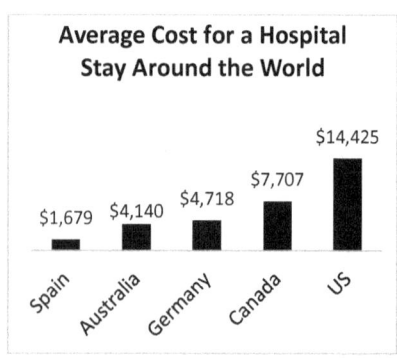

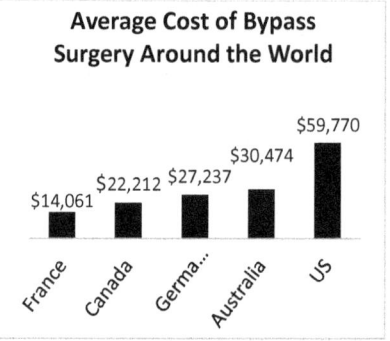

Why Healthcare is not a Commodity

Commodity: A raw material or primary agricultural product that can be turned to commercial advantage. A product as distinguished from a service that is interchangeable with other commodities of the same type.

The fundamental issue with healthcare and industry is that public health should not be viewed as a commodity, it is a public utility. In other words, public health is a community responsibility because the effects of poor health are directly reflected back to that community. When someone has a medical emergency they receive medical attention whether they've paid, or can pay, into the system or not. This negates the ability of the market to naturally regulate the price and value of health services. No matter how high the demand, the supply must be manipulated to meet it. This creates a very vulnerable situation for the working class. It places wellbeing on the opposing end of immediate profit, which in turn results in a higher cost of healthcare for the individual and the community when the neglected party has to undergo more invasive and costly procedures that preventative care might have eliminated.

How the Cost of Healthcare is Calculated

The cost of healthcare is defined as the total amount of dollars spent meeting the demand created in a given population. What that means is all the production costs for every facet of our healthcare system; the cost of a procedure, the salary of the health professional performing it, the chairs in the waiting room, the money spent on advertising, hospital administration etc. All of these variables come into play when assessing the value of health services. The reason this does not work in a for-profit system is that the value of a service is not always accurately appraisable. For example, heart surgery does not always prevent one from needing another surgery so while the cost of this type of surgery could be a hundred thousand dollars, it may not be economically "worth" that amount. An estimated 60% of all personal bankruptcies in America point to medical bills and of those cases 75% had medical insurance.

*"The doctor has been taught to be interested not in health but in disease. What the public is taught is that health is the cure for disease." - **Ashley Montagu**, Anthropologist, Princeton University*

The Scheme to Cover the Healthy and Lucrative

The most important cost saving healthcare practice is preventative care. The system saves money when we catch disease early and when people have access to a doctor to learn about safe health practices concerning their own unique condition. In America before the Affordable Care Act (Obamacare), we had a system with extremely limited access resulting in a very costly, unhealthy population. Not only does this drive up the total cost of healthcare, it defaults the burden onto the working-consumer class, and it was designed that way. The insurance companies, as a private extension of the government in charge of overseeing healthcare, strategized to cover the healthiest and most profitable candidates by disqualifying people in the most need with pre-existing conditions, choosing which procedures were allowable, and creating exclusive networks to tie-up the better doctors which ultimately restricts access.

"Health cannot be a question of income; it is a fundamental human right" - ***Nelson Mandela***, *Philanthropist and Revolutionary*

Understanding What Obamacare Accomplished

While the Affordable Care Act was not a perfect deal, it did force the insurance system to address the actual liability of our total health expenditure. While the healthy, previously insured population saw an increase in their premiums, an estimated 17 million people received coverage for the first time. Children 13 years and younger received healthcare automatically, young adults 24 and under could stay on their parents plan, pre-existing conditions could no longer disqualify a candidate, and anyone that could not afford a plan had to pay a fee to help offset the cost of covering the uninsured. In a time where corporate control had free reign to profit from the well being of the country, a mandate that held insurance companies responsible to assess the actual cost of healthcare was critical even though some have criticized it as furthering an already fascist operation. The Next step is a single-payer system that facilitates a public heath utility for all Americans and restricts private insurance to a luxury market.

Religion: Enemy of Progress

Scientific Oppression

Galileo Galilei – Theorized that the earth revolved around the sun; arrested. ᛣ

Muhammad Rhazes – Medical pioneer; beaten blind

Gerhard Domagk – Discovered the first commercially available antibiotic; arrested.

Cecco d'Ascoli – Astrologer and mathematician; burned alive.

Boethius – Philosopher; executed.

François de La Mothe Le Vayer - French writer, teacher and thinker; burned at the stake.

Giordano Bruno - Italian philosopher, mathematician and astronomer; burned at the stake.

Andreas Vesalius – World famous anatomist and physician; sentenced to death..

Giordano Bruno – Theorized the earth rotates around the sun; burnt at the stake.

Hypatia of Alexandria – Female philosopher and mathematician; murdered.

Henry Oldenburg – Published scientific papers from around the world; arrested.

Michael Servetus - Discovered pulmonary circulation; tortured and burned at the stake.

Since the dawn of time people have fabricated stories to explain things unexplainable, or more sinisterly, to prop up a political agenda. Millions have been persecuted, outcast, and oppressed in the name of myth. Listed above are only a few of the greatest thinkers in human history that were silenced by religious ignorance. Now, even with all our progress in science, the world still burns with turmoil over which ancient Middle Eastern scripture is the true key to humanity's morality and origin. Christianity, Islam, and Judaism are only the trendiest versions

16

of typical theism with similar plots and characters. There is even much confusion among the religious populations on whether or not the Islamic god, "Allah" is in fact the same god worshipped by Christians and Jews. This is of course true as all are Abrahamic religions. Without getting into too much criticism of particular theisms, I wanted to present the case to move away from faith to embrace wonder, discovery and science; the religion of enlightenment.

Terrorism

Proxy War: a war instigated by a major power that does not itself become involved.

Innocent people of good intention all over the world are held responsible for the actions of their radical counterparts, igniting a vicious cycle of justification for retaliation that never ends. Meanwhile, in the battle for land and increasingly limited natural resources, foreign governments battle radical religious militants funded or influenced by major world powers in proxy wars that purposefully obscure the truth from the casual voter. The most important thing to remember is that any centrally organized, rigid ideology coupled with civil unrest due to limited freedom or resources is an incubator for terrorism. There are even radical Buddhist monks (considered a mostly peaceful religion) that have terrorized regions of Myanmar and Thailand. Right now, world powers are employing radical religious factions to gain political authority and control of resources while the polarized but mostly civil inhabitants pay for it with their lives and personal liberties.

Freedom from Religion

Regardless of the atrocities stemming from religious conquest and the oppression of scientific thinkers, religion in our society places all of our personal liberty at risk. The Founding Fathers understood the importance of separating church and state and it wasn't until the 1950s that "Under God" was added to the Pledge of Allegiance, shortly thereafter; the motto "In God We Trust" was adopted as well, further encouraging the assumption that America is a Christian Nation. Consequentially, we have had a very difficult battle for the right to professional abortion, same-sex marriage and impartial education. This moves us further away from the ideas of libertarianism. Americans are easily targeted as the aggressors of religious conquest regardless of our diverse and independent perspectives

We must fight for everyone's freedom from any ideology, as much as we wish not to be oppressed by ideas we find foreign.

The Mental Box

Religion promotes a very old, and one dimensional view of our universe that restricts the realm of possibility and divisively separates human cultures. Fear of death is a defense mechanism biologically programmed within each of us, and while myth is the obvious compensation for fate and origins unknown, organized religion is the intentional exploitation of that fear. The belief in the traditional afterlife held by most religions is not only scientifically illogical, it devalues the immediate importance of life, and it fictionalizes the human spirit.

"Science is not only compatible with spirituality; it is a profound source of spirituality. When we recognize our place in an immensity of light-years and in the passage of ages, when we grasp the intricacy, beauty, and subtlety of life, then that soaring feeling, that sense of elation and humility combined, is surely spiritual." – Carl Sagan, Astronomer, Harvard University

Racism: Byproduct of Social and Economic Inequality

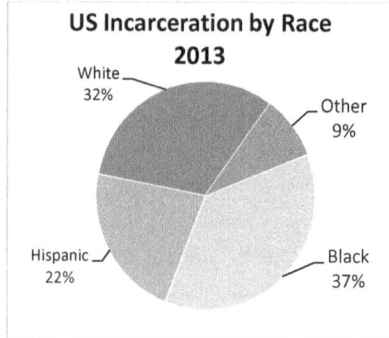

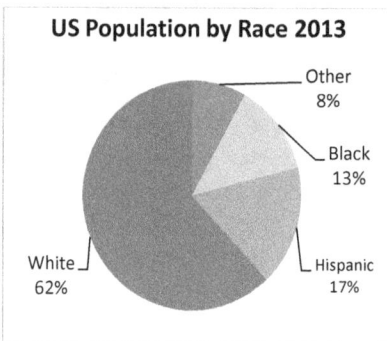

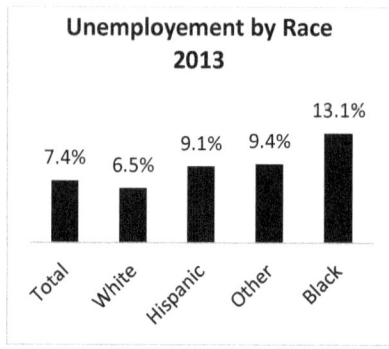

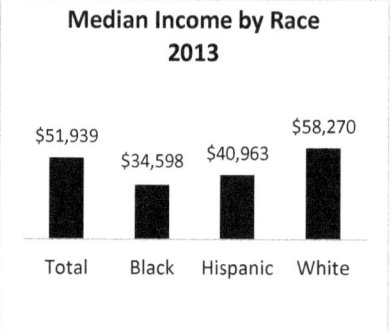

Segregationists

The greatest difference between fascist and communist social structures is that while they both do not protect personal liberties over national interests by design, fascist regimes operate under exclusionary policies for the encouragement of industry and the success of society. Through discriminatory social policies they suppress the population that isn't appointed social priority. Communism on the other hand, is overly inclusive and anyone can be deemed a threat to the state. Again, we can look at Nazi Germany as an example of racial segregation, and the practice of the pseudoscience known as "scientific racism". The Nazis believed that by eliminating diversity within the social structure, economic and cultural prosperity could be achieved. The Aryan race, or "master race" as Hitler defined it, was thought to be the only race worthy of life and that the other races were parasitic. While this was a very drastic and primitive way of thinking, the same thought pattern relates to social Darwinism and it manifests in modern times as more of a class hierarchy where the lower classes are characterized as lazy and parasitic on society because they may collect food stamps or live in government housing. However, as we discussed earlier, some of these things may be beyond an individual's control. Throughout world history racism has affected people of all ethnicities and America is no different.

How Social Darwinism Promotes Racism

Social Darwinism: The application of Darwinism (Survival of the Fittest) to a society; specifically a theory in sociology that individuals or groups achieve advantage over others as the result of genetic or biological superiority.

Fundamentally, Social Darwinism is the conservative strategy for the success of a society. Where liberals believe that a society's success is based not only on economic growth but some amount of economic equality within that growth, the conservative angle favors economic growth at the expense of the "weak" or "unworthy". In any community though, the selection of the elite (or "winners") and the working class (or "losers") has not, and cannot be naturally judicious. There are many factors that determine economic advantage. While some advantages are natural and measurable most of the time it's where you live, who you know, what college you can afford, inheritance, etc that determines ones advantage, and this is almost always intertwined with cultural differences and historical bias.

Institutional Racism

As you can see in the previous charts, while minorities made up only 38% of the US population in 2013, they accounted for 68% of the imprisoned population. Realistically the cards are stacked against anyone from a social background that does not align itself within the accepted ideology of the state. The reactions to this reality cannot be predicted. Years of oppression and cultural division have created very polarizing perspectives on what are acceptable means for surviving in the American economic climate. A broken justice system, failed economy and cut-rate education system only sustain the corruption almost subconsciously as our institutions are merely a reflection of ourselves.

"I think that we've got to see that a riot is the language of the unheard. And, what is it that America has failed to hear? It has failed to hear that the economic plight of the Negro poor has worsened over the last few years." – Martin Luther King Junior, Civil Rights Activist and Humanitarian

White Privilege Explained

Economic disparity continues to exaggerate racial differences in the United States. White people disproportionately have economic or social advantages that are hard to pinpoint but create very different perspectives and obstacles for minorities. This is not to say there aren't whites with similar perspectives as disadvantaged minorities, or inversely, that there aren't minorities from the economically elite perspective either, which further obscures the distinction of this observable truth. It is very easy to see statistically that minorities have a greater chance of going to jail, and a harder time getting a job. The reasons why, however, are difficult for someone without the same obstacles to understand. While a white person in an economically healthy area may just be lazy for being unemployed, a black person may be living in an area where there aren't as many opportunities or what opportunities are available may be drastically less advantageous. This contrast of perspectives creates a racial tension, fueled by misunderstanding, when we question the motives, lifestyle or political outlook of someone from a different social background.

"Let us understand that when we stand together, we will always win. When men and women stand together for justice, we win. When black, white and Hispanic people stand together for justice, we win." – Bernie Sanders, Independent Senator and Civil Rights Activist

The Corporate Media: Enemy of Democracy

Media Giants

News Corp	Time Warner
□ Fox	□ CNN
□ Wall Street Journal	□ HBO
□ New York Post	□ TIME
□ 130+ Newspapers	□ TMZ
□ National Geographic	□ DC Comics
□ Dow Jones & Company	□ Warner Brothers
Disney	**Viacom**
□ ABC	□ MTV
□ ESPN	□ BET
□ Lucasfilm	□ CMT
□ Marvel	□ Paramount
□ Touchstone Pictures	□ Nickelodeon
Comcast	**CBS**
□ General Electric	□ Showtime
□ NBC	□ Smithsonian
□ Universal	□ Westinghouse
□ Telemundo	□ 100+ Radio Stations
Bain Capital	**Cox Enterprises**
□ IHeartMedia Group	□ 86 Radio Stations
□ Clear Channel Communications	□ 15 TV Stations
□ 800+ Radio Stations	□ Autotrader
□ 1 Million Billboards in 30 countries	□ Kelley Blue Book
Tegna Inc	**Hearst Corporation**
□ Gannett Company	□ A&E
□ USA Today	□ 20+ Magazines
□ 100+ Newspapers	□ 16 Newspapers
□ 40+ TV Stations	□ 30+ TV Stations
National Public Radio (NPR)	**Advance Publications**
□ 900 Radio Stations	□ 30+ Newspapers
□ All Things Considered	□ BrightHouse Networks
□ Morning Edition	□ Discovery Channel

Long Lost Heroes

One of the most vital balances in any democratic community is journalism; individuals seeking truth through investigation and analysis with nonpartisan motive. America has completely lost all transparency in the media and it's a huge obstacle in our quest to reinstall liberty. In 1983, 90% of the media in the United States was controlled by 50 different organizations, today only a handful remain. Those same companies also own, invest in, or distribute similar outlets across the world creating an information oligopoly that controls almost every newspaper, television program and radio broadcast in the world. Through the influence of the cronyists in the shadow oligarchy they purposefully confuse the population to vote against their interests with selective reporting and instigating perpetual conflict. This corruption speaks for itself. How can we elevate authentic political consciousness with the monopoly that is the corporate media?

"The media's the most powerful entity on earth. They have the power to make the innocent guilty and to make the guilty innocent, and that's power, because they control the minds of the masses." – Malcolm X, Human Rights Activist

The New Media

With the domination of established media outlets, a new breed of vigilante journalism in the form of whistle blowers, hacktivists and internet reporters have emerged. The World Wide Web has made instant communication possible and information harder to suppress. Controversial heroes like Edward Snowden, Coleen Rowley, Sherron Watkins, and Bradley Manning; Infamous entities like Anonymous, Wiki Leaks and the Chaos Computer Club are just some of the new protectors of democracy in the digital age. We must stand in support of these martyrs and deny the corporate media if we wish to achieve transparency in the war for our minds.

"There can be no faith in government if our highest offices are excused from scrutiny - they should be setting the example of transparency." - Edward Snowden, NSA Whistleblower

How We Can Revive Democracy

The time has come in America for a renaissance. A shadow oligarchy controls every facet of our society, from who we vote for, to how our children are educated, and ultimately, the amount of liberty we can enjoy. While voter turnout has diminished due to voter suppression and a general distrust in the political system altogether, the Citizens United ruling has allowed anyone with enough money to purchase influence in our government. Disenfranchised factions of the radical left and right are reeling against each other, fueled by persuasive confusion propagated by the corporate media. I hope this guide has given you a transparent foundation on which you can form your own opinions about what you can do to influence the direction of our future. While it is easy to jump to conclusions in the face of adversity, we must all understand that cultural issues and the political exploitation of people caught on either side happens in cycles and is repeated throughout history as a method of control. The influence of propaganda is an immensely powerful, universal force that has tightened its grip on information outlets worldwide in an attempt to win the war for our minds. We must strive for nonpartisan compromise and refuse to be politically separated. I believe, much like the great American revolutionaries, that if we come together and elevate political consciousness with well organized activism and open-minded discussion we can create a community that works for all of us, we can shed the ideological constructs working against humanity that stifles our cultural progress, and we can revive a new "American Dream". Support local industry, stay involved in all local and national elections, and actively engage people in civil conversation.

*"Extremes to the right and to the left of any political dispute are always wrong." – **Dwight D. Eisenhower**, 34th President of the United States*

<u>Glossary</u>

Administration: the officials in the executive branch of government under a particular chief executive.

Agenda: the underlying intentions or motives of a particular person or group.

Anarchism: a political philosophy that advocates self-governed societies with voluntary institutions.

Aryan race: A racial group commonly used to describe people of European and Western Asian heritage. While originally meant as a neutral classification, it has been used by supremacists and segregational organizations.

Authoritarian: of or relating to a governmental or political system, principle, or practice in which individual freedom is held as completely subordinate to the power or authority of the state, centered either in one person or a small group that is not constitutionally accountable to the people.

Capital: wealth in the form of money or other assets owned by a person or organization or available or contributed for a particular purpose such as starting a company or investing.

Capitalism: an economic system characterized by private or corporate ownership of capital goods.

Catalyst: a person or event that quickly causes change or action.

Civil discourse: engagement in conversation intended to enhance understanding.

Commodity: a raw material or primary agricultural product that can be turned to commercial advantage. A product as distinguished from a service that is interchangeable with other commodities of the same type.

Communism: a left-wing system of social organization in which all economic and social activity is controlled by a totalitarian state dominated by a single and self-perpetuating political party.

Cronyism: the appointment of friends and associates to positions of authority or opportunity, without proper regard to their qualifications.

Democracy: government by the people; a form of government in which the supreme power is vested in the people and exercised directly by them or by their elected agents under a free electoral system.

Fascism: an authoritarian and nationalistic right-wing system of government that through indirect control of a community by an elite group of private ownership owns the means to production and typically uses exclusive social policy.

Fiat Money: inconvertible paper money made legal tender by government decree.

Hacktivism: activism by gaining unauthorized access to a computer system and carrying out various disruptive demonstrations as a means of achieving political or social goals.

Inflation: a general increase in prices and fall in the purchasing value of money.

Judicious: having, exercising, or characterized by good or discriminating judgment; wise, sensible, or well-advised discretion.

Laissez-faire: a policy, or attitude, of letting things take their own course without interference.

Libertarianism: a political philosophy that upholds liberty as its principle objective.

Lobbyist: a person who takes part in an organized attempt to influence legislators.

Martyr: a person who sacrifices something of great value and especially life itself for the sake of principle.

Monopolization: to obtain exclusive possession of.

Oligarchy: a small group that exercises control especially for corrupt and selfish purposes in any type of government.

Oligopoly: A state of limited competition, in which a market is shared and controlled by a small number of producers.

Oppression: the state of being subject to unjust treatment or control.

Polarized Pluralism: is a description applied to a two-party or multi-party political system which is seen as overly polarized and therefore as dysfunctional.

Propaganda: information, especially of a biased or misleading nature, used to promote or publicize a particular political cause or point of view.

Proxy War: a war instigated by a major power that does not itself become involved.

Scientific Racism: the use of scientific techniques and hypotheses to support or justify the belief in racism, racial inferiority, or racial superiority.

Social Darwinism: the application of Darwinism (survival of the fittest) to the study of human society, specifically, a theory in sociology that individuals or groups achieve advantage over others as the result of genetic or biological superiority.

Special Interest Group: a person or group seeking to influence legislative or government policy to further narrowly defined interests.

Utopia: is a community or society possessing highly desirable or near perfect qualities.

Special Thanks:

Colin Jones Jr.	John Alexander	Daniel Diaz
Chris Hooper	Charlene Ringo	Jordan Cole
Bear Seemann	Vinny Acerra	Ian Rouleau
Pamela Intartaglia	Stephanie Salazar	Justin Lundy
Courtney Hogue	Melissa Deem	Zach Craigmile
Shannon Ledbetter	Tonya Ringo	Tracy Intartaglia

Without these people, this book would not be possible. Thank you.

www.ingramcontent.com/pod-product-compliance
Lightning Source LLC
Chambersburg PA
CBHW061945280526
45787CB00004B/1732